D0324353

A Gift for:

_____

From:

_____

MERRY CHRISTMAS

with Love

CHRIS SHEA

COUNTRYMAN

Copyright © 2003 by Chris Shea. DBA Lifesighs Cards, PO Box 19446,
San Diego, CA 92159. All rights reserved. Represented by Linda McDonald, Inc.,
Charlotte, North Carolina.

Published by J. Countryman, a division of Thomas Nelson, Inc, Nashville,
Tennessee 37214.

Project manager: Terri Gibbs

No portion of this publication may be reproduced, stored in a retrieval system
or transmitted in any form by any means—electronic, mechanical, photocopying,
recording, or any other—except for brief quotations in printed reviews, without
the prior written permission of the publisher.

Cover design by Robin Black, UDG | Designworks, Sisters, Oregon.

ISBN: 1-4041-0013-X

www.jcountryman.com
www.thomasnelson.com

Printed and bound in the United States of America

For my mother Helen Givens

God has blessed us
forever.

That is what Christmas
is
all
about.

The nature of Christmas

is

giving...

because it all began
with
a
Gift.

A gift that
can only
be
received,

a gift
that brought
Joy
to the world,

a Gift

that

came

special delivery.

As promised,

God sent His Best,

and the sky and the stars

gave the world's first baby shower.

(God knew they
couldn't afford
announcements

So He lent them
a
star,

...the only Nightlight

with a lifetime guarantee.)

Christmas
has a
radiance
all its
own

and even unplugged
        could illuminate
            the world.

(Two-thousand years later

(God leaves the Light on still.)

God revealed
a
glimpse
of
Heaven
that night
in
the manger;

the setting was humble
and the cast was divine.

Then
through a tiny door
    every creature saw it,
        the
    enormous
        gift
        of

    eternal Love,

and all who
entered
knew they stood
upon

the very floor
of
Heaven.

This was the
touch
of
Christmas:

the simple
became the sacred.

Even the World's
first
Masterpiece

was only framed
in straw.

Who but
God
would think
of
Sending a Message

and wrapping it in swaddling clothes?

Who but
   God
Knew it would take
  the
  heart of a
      Child

to reach
    the
    soul
        of the world?

God is Love.

Christmas is proof:

for only from
the
heart of God
could
such a one
as Jesus
come...

such a
    tiny
        little
            son

who would
grow to comfort
        all
        the
        World,

a Savior
to
look up to

who would never
look
down
on us.

Jesus . . .

our best,
our ever friend.

Peace on earth
began
in a manger,

the Christmas Presence
asleep in the
hay.

May the
simple
beauty of
Christmas

take your breath

away.

May you taste
the love
in every
Christmas cookie,

hear joy
    in every

  Christmas song,

feel warmth
in
every
Christmas
present;

and

in the midst of all the

celebration,

may you make room for
Peace.

Merry Christmas With Love